KEEPSAKES

AUTUMN

First published in the United States by
Salem House Publishers, 462 Boston Street,
Topsfield, Massachusetts, 01983.

Copyright © Swallow Publishing Ltd 1988

Conceived and produced by
Swallow Publishing Ltd, Swallow House,
11-21 Northdown Street, London N1 9BN

ISBN: 0 88162 342 3
Art Director: Elaine Partington
Designer: Jean Hoyes
Printed in Hong Kong by Imago Publishing Limited

KEEPSAKES

AUTUMN

Compiled by
Samantha Younger

Salem House

After the Harvest

I N THE AUTUMN after the harvest the gleaning is still an important time to the cottager, though nothing like it used to be. Reaping by machinery has made rapid inroads, and there is not nearly so much left behind as in former days. Yet half the women and children of the place go out and glean, but very few now bake at home; they have their bread from the baker, who comes round in the smallest hamlets. Possibly they had a more wholesome article in the olden time, when the wheat from their gleanings was ground at the village mill, and the flour made into bread at home. But the cunning of the mechanician has invaded the ancient customs; the very sheaves are now to be bound with wire by the same machine that reaps the corn.

THE GREAT PAINTER, Autumn, has just touched with the tip of his brush a branch of the beech-tree, here and there leaving an orange spot, and the green acorns are tinged with a faint yellow. The hedges, perfect mines of beauty, look almost red from a distance, so innumerable are the peggles.

RICHARD JEFFERIES

Departure of Autumn

Autumn departs, but still his mantle's fold
   Rests on the groves of noble Somerville.
Beneath a shroud of russet dropped with gold
   Tweed and his tributaries mingle still.
Hoarser the wind, and deeper sounds the rill,
   Yet lingering notes of silvan music swell,
The deep-toned cushat, and the redbreast shrill;
   And yet some tints of summer splendour tell
When the broad sun sinks down on Ettrick's western fell.

Autumn departs. From Gala's fields no more
   Come rural sounds our kindred banks to cheer;
Blent with the stream, and gale that wafts it o'er,
   No more the distant reaper's mirth we hear.

SIR WALTER SCOTT

There is a harmony in autumn,
   and a lustre in its sky,
Which through the summer
   is not heard or seen.

PERCY BYSSHE SHELLEY

Nature's New Look

The feathers of the willow
    Are half of them grown yellow
Above the swelling stream.
    And ragged are the bushes,
And rusty are the rushes,
    And wild the clouded gleam.
The thistle now is older,
    His stalk begins to moulder,
His head is white as snow.
    The branches all are barer,
The linnet's song is rarer,
    The robin pipeth now.

RICHARD WATSON DIXON

Fall, leaves, fall; die, flowers, away.
    Lengthen night and shorten day.
Every leaf speaks bliss to me,
    Fluttering from the autumn tree.
I shall smile when wreaths of snow
    Blossom where the rose should grow.
I shall sing when night's decay
    Ushers in a drearier day.

EMILY BRONTE

A Stormy Day

SEPTEMBER 19TH. The wind grumbled and made itself miserable all last night, and this morning it is still howling as ill-naturedly as ever, and roaring and rumbling in the chimneys. The tide is far out, but from an upper window, I fancied, at intervals, that I could see the plash of the surf-wave on the distant limit of the sand; perhaps, however, it was only a gleam on the sky. Constantly there have been sharp spatters of rain, hissing and rattling against the windows, while a little before or after, or perhaps simultaneously, a rainbow, somewhat watery of texture, paints itself on the western clouds. Grey, sullen vapours hang about the sky, or sometimes cover it with a uniform dullness; at other times, the portions towards the sun gleam almost lightsomely; now, there may be an airy glimpse of clear blue sky in a fissure of the clouds; now, the very brightest of sunshine comes out all of a sudden, and gladdens everything. The breadth of sands has a various aspect, according as there are pools, or moisture enough to glisten; or a drier tract; and where the light gleams along a yellow ridge or bar, it is like sunshine itself. Certainly the temper of the day shifts; but the smiles come far the seldomest, and its frowns and angry tears are most reliable.

NATHANIEL HAWTHORNE

Summer's Flight

I at my window sit, and see
    Autumn his russet fingers lay
On every leaf of every tree.
    I call, but Summer will not stay.

She flies, the boasting goddess flies,
    And, pointing where the espaliers shoot,
'Deserve my parting gift,' she cries,
    'I take the leaves but not the fruit.'

Let me the parting gift improve
    And emulate the just reply,
As life's short seasons swift remove,
    Ere fixed in Winter's frost I lie.

Health, beauty, vigour now decline,
    The pride of Summer's splendid day,
Leaves, which the stem must now resign,
    The mournful prelude of decay.

But let fair Virtue's fruit remain,
    Though Summer with my leaves be fled.
Then, not despised, I'll not complain,
    But cherish Autumn in her stead.

ANONYMOUS, 18TH CENTURY

Notes from a Journal

SEPTEMBER 2ND 1789. Bees feed on the plums and the mellow gooseberries. They often devour the peaches and nectarines.

September 6th. Fog, sun, pleasant showers, moonshine. Rain in the night. Mushrooms begin to come . . . .

September 9th. Hops are not large. The flycatchers, which abounded in my outlet, seem to have withdrawn themselves. Some grapes begin to turn colour. Men bind wheat. Sweet harvest and hop-picking weather. Hirundines congregate on barns and trees and on the tower. The hops are smaller than they were last year. There is fine clover in many fields.

September 13th. After a bright night and vast dew the sky usually becomes clouded by eleven or twelve o'clock in the forenoon, and clear again towards the decline of the day. The reason seems to be that the dew, drawn up by evaporation, occasions the clouds, which towards evening, being no longer rendered buoyant by the warmth of the sun, melt away and fall down again in dews. If clouds are watched of a still, warm evening, they will be seen to melt away and disappear. Several nests of goldfinches, with fledged young, were found among the vines of the hops.

GILBERT WHITE

The Fitful Wind

I love the fitful gust that shakes
    The casement all the day,
And from the glossy elm tree takes
    The faded leaves away,
Twirling them by the window pane
With thousand others down the lane.

I love to see the shaking twig
    Dance till shut of eve,
The sparrow on the cottage rig,
    Whose chirp would make believe
That Spring was just now flirting by
In Summer's lap with flowers to lie.

I love to see the cottage smoke
    Curl upwards through the trees;
The pigeons nestled round the cote
    On November days like these;
The cock upon the dunghill crowing,
The mill sails on the heath a-going.

JOHN CLARE

Timely Advice

Thresh seed and to fanning, September doth crie,
  get plough to the field, and be sowing of rie.
To harrow the rydgis, er ever ye strike,
  is one peece of husbandrie Suffolk doth like.

Sowe timely thy whitewheat, sowe rie in the dust,
  let seede have his longing, let soile have hir lust.
Let rie be partaker of Mihelmas spring,
  to beare out the hardnes that winter doth bring.

Though beanes be in sowing but scattered in,
  yet wheat, rie, and peason, I love not too thin.
Sowe barlie and dredge, with a plentifull hand,
  least weede, steed of seede, over groweth thy land.

No sooner a sowing, but out by and by,
  with mother or boy that alarum can cry
and let them be armed with sling or with bowe,
  to skare any piggen, the rooke and the crowe.

The barbery, respis, and goosebery too,
  looke now to be planted as other things doo.
The goosebery, respis, and roses, al three,
  with strawberies under them trimly agree.

THOMAS TUSSER

The First Thanksgiving

AFTERWARDS THEY (as many as were able) began to plant their corn, in which service Squanto stood them in great stead, showing them both the manner how to set it, and after how to dress and tend it. Also he told them except they got fish and set with it in these old grounds it would come to nothing . . . all which they found true by trial and experience . . . .

They began now to gather in the small harvest they had, and to fit up their houses and dwellings against winter, being all well recovered in health and strength, and had all things in good plenty. For as some were thus employed in affairs abroad, others were exercised in fishing, about cod and bass and other fish . . . of which every family had their portion. All the summer there was no want.

And now began to come in store of fowl, as winter approached, of which this place did abound when they came first (but afterward decreased by degrees). And besides waterfowl there was great store of wild turkeys, of which they took many besides venison, etc. Besides they had about a peck a meal a week to a person, or now since harvest, Indian corn to that proportion – which made many afterwards write so largely of their plenty here to their friends in England.

WILLIAM BRADFORD, 1621

Ode to Autumn

Season of mists and mellow fruitfulness,
    Close bosom-friend of the maturing sun;
Conspiring with him how to load and bless
    With fruit the vines that round the thatch-eaves run;
    To bend with apples the mossed cottage-trees,
    And fill all fruit with ripeness to the core;
      To swell the gourd, and plump the hazel shells
    With a sweet kernel; to set budding more,
    And still more, later flowers for the bees,
    Until they think warm days will never cease,
      For Summer has o'er-brimmed their clammy cells –

Who hath not seen thee oft amid thy store?
    Sometimes whoever seeks abroad may find
Thee sitting careless on a granary floor,
    Thy hair soft-lifted by the winnowing wind;
Or on a half-reaped furrow sound asleep,
    Drowsed with the fume of poppies, while thy hook
      Spares the next swath and all its twinèd flowers.
And sometimes like a gleaner thou dost keep
    Steady thy laden head across a brook;
    Or by a cyder-press, with patient look,
      Thou watchest the last oozings hours by hours.

JOHN KEATS

October Days

HERE ARE DAYS which occur in this climate, at almost any season of the year, wherein the world reaches its perfection, when the air, the heavenly bodies, and the earth, make a harmony, as if nature would indulge her offspring;...when everything that has life gives sign of satisfaction, and the cattle that lie on the ground seem to have great and tranquil thoughts. These halcyons may be looked for with a little more assurance in that pure October weather, which we distinguish by the name of the Indian Summer. The day, immeasurably long, sleeps over the broad hills and warm wide fields. To have lived through all its sunny hours seems longevity enough.

RALPH WALDO EMERSON

IT IS NOW OCTOBER, and the lofty winds bare the trees of their leaves, while the hogs in the woods grow fat on fallen acorns ....The hare on the hill makes a fair meal for the greyhound, and the fox in the woods calls the hounds to full cry. Kind hearts and true lovers lie close to keep off the cold. The titmouse now remains in the hollow of a tree and the blackbird takes refuge in the bottom of a hedge.

NICHOLAS BRETON

Hay stacks dont always
stay on shore .

September in the Garden

EPTEMBER To be done in the orchard and olitory garden: Gather now (if ripe) your winter fruits as apples, pears, plums etc, to prevent their falling by the great winds. Also gather your wind-falls from day to day; do this work in dry weather. Sow lettuce, radish, spinage, parsneps, cauly-flowers, cabbage, onions etc. Sow also winter herbs and roots, and plant strawberries out of the woods. No longer now defer the taking of your bees, streightening the entrances of such hives as you leave to a small passage, and continue still your hostility against wasps and other robbing insects. Cider-making continues.

To be done in the parterre, and flower garden. Plant some of all the sorts of anemonies after the first rains, if you will have flowers very forwards; but it is surer to attend till October or the month after, lest the over moisture of the autumnal seasons give you cause to repent. Begin now also to plant some tulips, unless you will stay until the later end of October, to prevent all hazard of rotting the bulbs. . . . Bind up now your autumnal flowers and plants to stakes, to prevent sudden gusts which will else prostrate all you have so industriously raised.

DION CLAYTON CALTHROP

Colours Rich
and Glorious

There is a beautiful spirit breathing now
   Its mellow richness on the clustered trees,
And, from a beaker full of richest dyes,
   Pouring new glory on the autumn woods,
And dipping in warm light the pillared clouds.
   Morn on the mountain, like a summer bird,
Lifts up her purple wing, and in the vales
   The gentle wind, a sweet and passionate wooer,
Kisses the blushing leaf, and stirs up life
   Within the solemn woods of ash deep-crimsoned,
And silver beech, and maple yellow-leaved,
   Where Autumn, like a faint old man, sits down
By the wayside a-weary.

HENRY WADSWORTH LONGFELLOW

No Spring, nor Summer beauty
   hath such grace
As I have seen
   in one Autumnal face.

JOHN DONNE

Seasonal Reflections

Early he rose, and looked with many a sigh
   On the red light that filled the eastern sky.
Oft had he stood before, alert and gay,
   To hail the glories of the new-born day.
But now dejected, languid, listless, low,
   He saw the wind upon the water blow,
And the cold stream curled onward as the gale
   From the pine-hill blew harshly down the dale.
On the right side the youth a wood surveyed,
   With all its dark intensity of shade,
Where the rough wind alone was heard to move,
   In this, the pause of nature and of love,
When now the young are reared, and when the old,
   Lost to the tie, grow negligent and cold.
Far to the left he saw the huts of men,
   Half hid in mist, that hung upon the fen.
Before him swallows, gathering for the sea,
   Took their short flights, and twittered on the lea,
And near the bean-sheaf stood, the harvest done,
   And slowly blackened in the sickly sun.
All these were sad in nature, or they took
   Sadness from him, the likeness of his look.

GEORGE CRABBE

"Autumn's mock sunshine of the faded woods"

Autumn Leaves

THE LEAVES HAVE lost their individuality, like a multitude of people on some calamitous day. Wild and reckless companies fly down the rides, beech and hornbeam, elm, ash and sycamore, in strangely assorted crowds – no longer in demure families, each on its own tree. The sound of their hurrying feet comes near, then with wild unreason they turn, desperately flying from the invisible. Before the old west wind that blows from the sunset, the wise wind that knew the Atlantic before a ship was on it, the strong wind that maddens the sea-horses, it is no wonder that the leaves are afraid. The very trees are bending double before it, groaning in the agony of their defiance. The lithe little birches sweep to earth in an ecstasy of surrender; the fir-trees lash themselves; the saplings have learnt obedience – their slender elasticity is at the wind's will; only the stiff old oaks and elms refuse to yield, and ominous crashes tell of their struggle. The live creatures of the wood have hidden from the tumult. The most living things in the place are the leaves; with their scurrying feet and their complaining, whispering voices, they are like an elfin nation, a lost tribe, a defeated army that has forgotten discipline.

MARY WEBB

Rural Repose

THE FALLEN LEAVES, with which the ground was strewn, gave forth a pleasant fragrance, and, subduing all harsh sounds of distant feet and wheels, created a repose in gentle unison with the light scattering of seed hither and thither by the distant husbandman, and with the noiseless passage of the plough as it turned up the rich brown earth and wrought a graceful pattern in the stubbled fields. On the motionless branches of some trees autumn berries hung like clusters of coral beads, as in those fabled orchards where the fruits were jewels; others, stripped of all their garniture, stood, each the centre of its little heap of bright red leaves, watching their slow decay; others again still wearing theirs, had them all crunched and crackled up, as though they had been burnt. About the stems of some were piled, in ruddy mounds, the apples they had borne that year; while others (hardy evergreens this class) showed somewhat stern and gloomy in their vigour . . . . Still athwart their darker boughs the sunbeams struck out paths of deeper gold; and the red light, mantling in among their swarthy branches, used them as foils to set its brightness off, and aid the lustre of the dying day.

CHARLES DICKENS

The End of Love

I loved my love from green of Spring
   Until sere Autumn's fall;
But now that leaves are withering
   How should one love at all?
One heart's too small
   For hunger, cold, love, everything.

I loved my love on sunny days
   Until late Summer's wane;
But now that frost begins to glaze
   How should one love again?
Nay, love and pain
   Walk wide apart in diverse ways.

I loved my love – alas to see
   That this should be, alas!
I thought that this could scarcely be,
   Yet has it come to pass:
Sweet sweet love was,
   Now bitter bitter grown to me.

CHRISTINA GEORGINA ROSSETTI

Shadows and Sighs

Summer is gone on swallows' wings,
    And Earth has buried all her flowers:
No more the lark, the linnet sings,
    But Silence sits in faded bowers.
There is a shadow on the plain
    Of Winter ere he comes again.
There is in woods a solemn sound
    Of hollow warnings whispered round,
As Echo in her deep recess
    For once had turned a prophetess.
Shuddering Autumn stops to list,
    And breathes his fear in sudden sighs,
With clouded face, and hazel eyes
    That quench themselves, and hide in mist.

THOMAS HOOD

John Peel's Song

D'ye ken John Peel with his coat so gay?
D'ye ken John Peel at the break of day?
D'ye ken John Peel when he's far, far away,
With his hounds and his horn in the morning?
    For the sound of his horn brought me from my bed,
    And the cry of his hounds which he oft-times led,
    Peel's view-halloo would awaken the dead,
    Or the fox from his lair in the morning.

Yes, I ken John Peel and Ruby too,
Ranter and Ringwood and Bellman and True;
From a find to a check, from a check to a view,
From a view to a death in the morning.

And I've followed John Peel both often and far
O'er the rasper-fence and the gate and the bar,
From Low Denton Holme up to Scratchmere Scar,
When we vied for the brush in the morning.
    For the sound of his horn brought me from my bed,
    And the cry of his hounds which he oft-times led,
    Peel's view-halloo would awaken the dead,
    Or the fox from his lair in the morning.

JOHN WOODCOCK GRAVES

The Redbreast

Driven in by autumn's sharpening air
   From half-stripped woods and pastures
     bare,
Brisk Robin seeks a kindlier home:
   Not like a beggar is he come,
But enters as a looked-for guest,
   Confiding in his ruddy breast,
As if it were a natural shield
   Charged with a blazon on the field,
Due to that good and pious deed
   Of which we in the ballad read.
But pensive fancies putting by,
   And wild-wood sorrows, speedily
He plays the expert ventriloquist;
   And, caught by glimpses now – now missed,
Puzzles the listener with a doubt
   If the soft voice he throws about
Comes from within doors or without!
   Was ever such a sweet confusion,
Sustained by delicate illusion?

WILLIAM WORDSWORTH

Sources and Acknowledgments

For permission to reproduce illustrations, the publishers thank the following: Mary Evans Picture Library, Spink & Son Ltd., Manchester City Art Galleries, the Mansell Collection and Sam Elder.